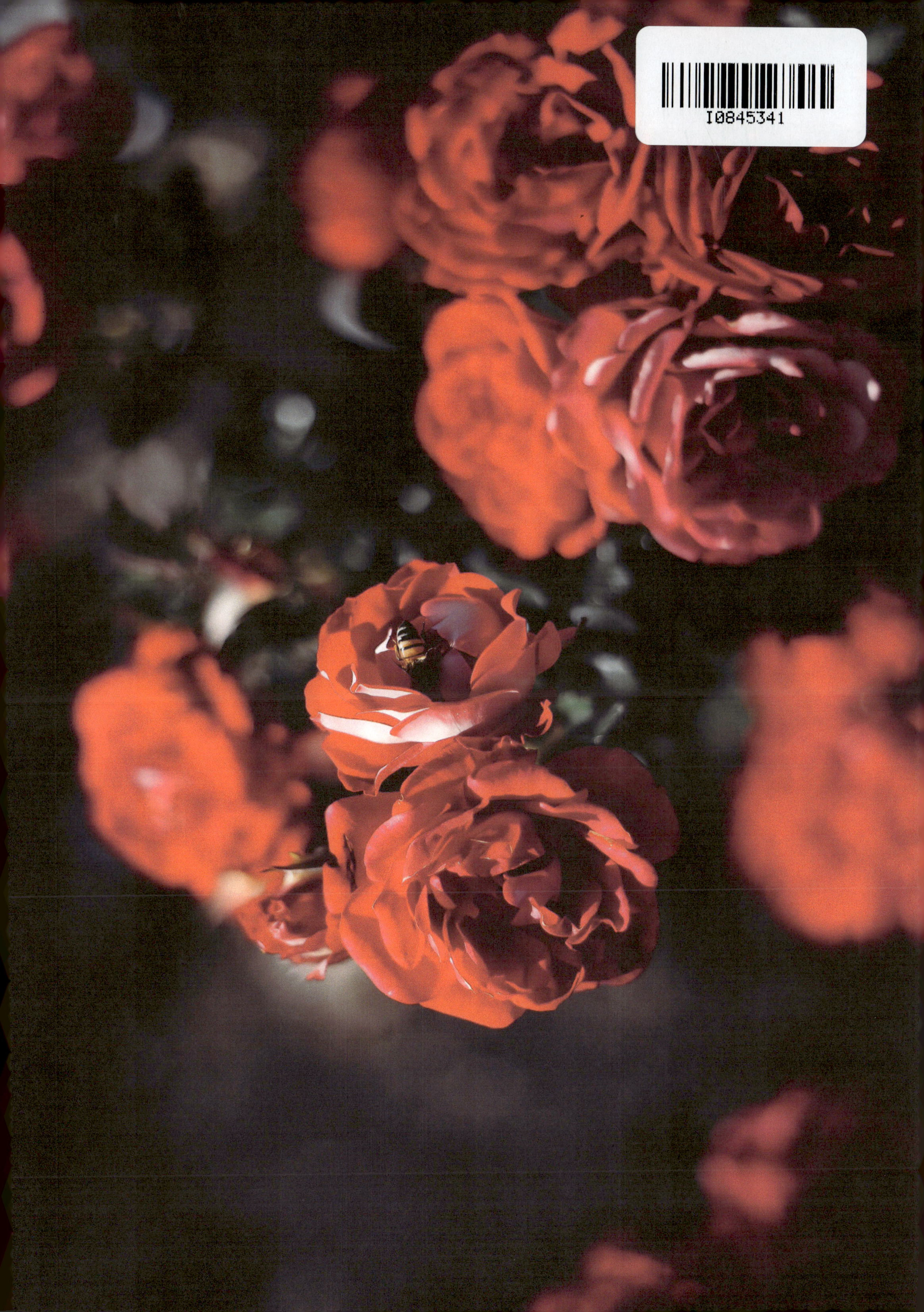

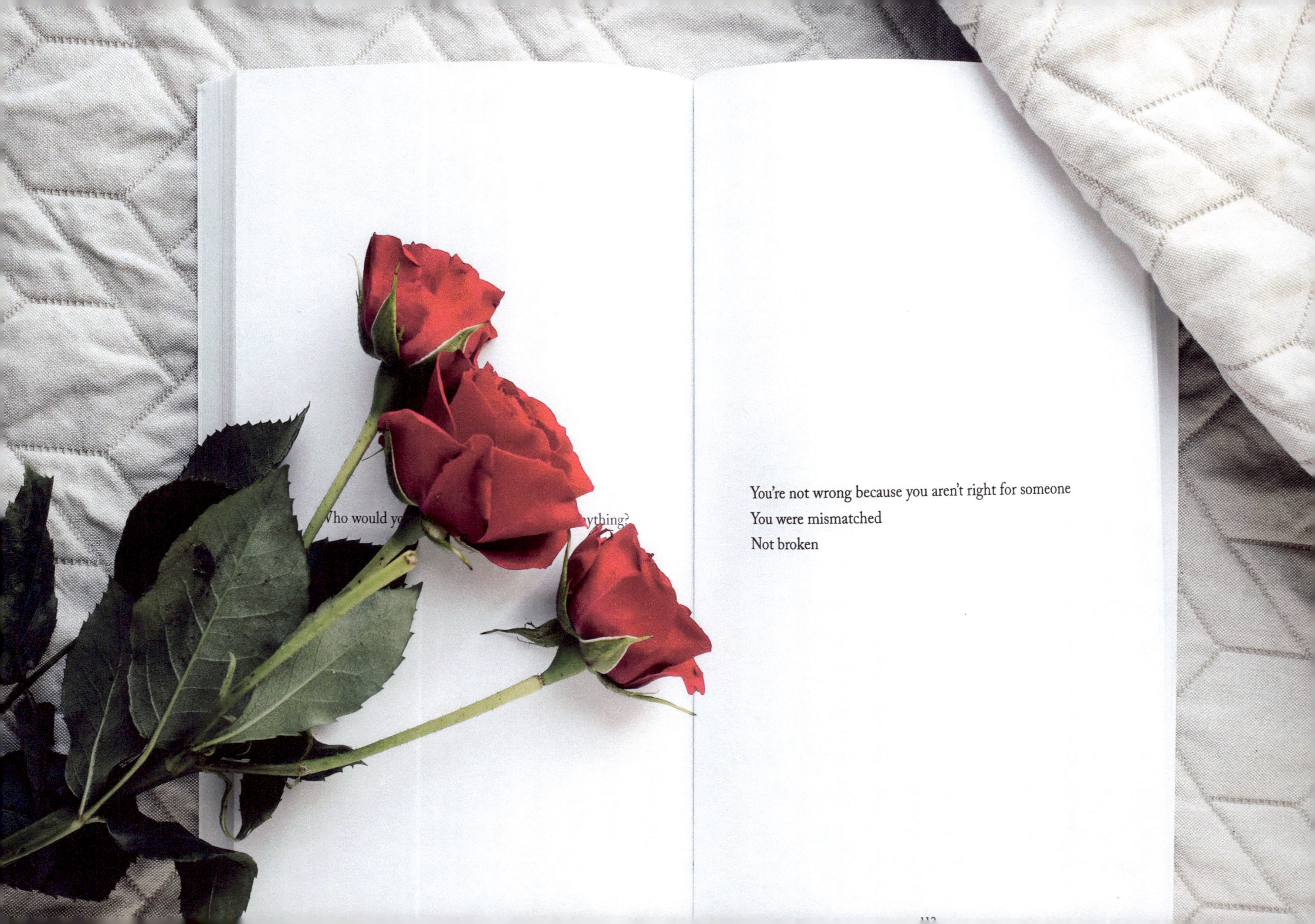

You're not wrong because you aren't right for someone
You were mismatched
Not broken

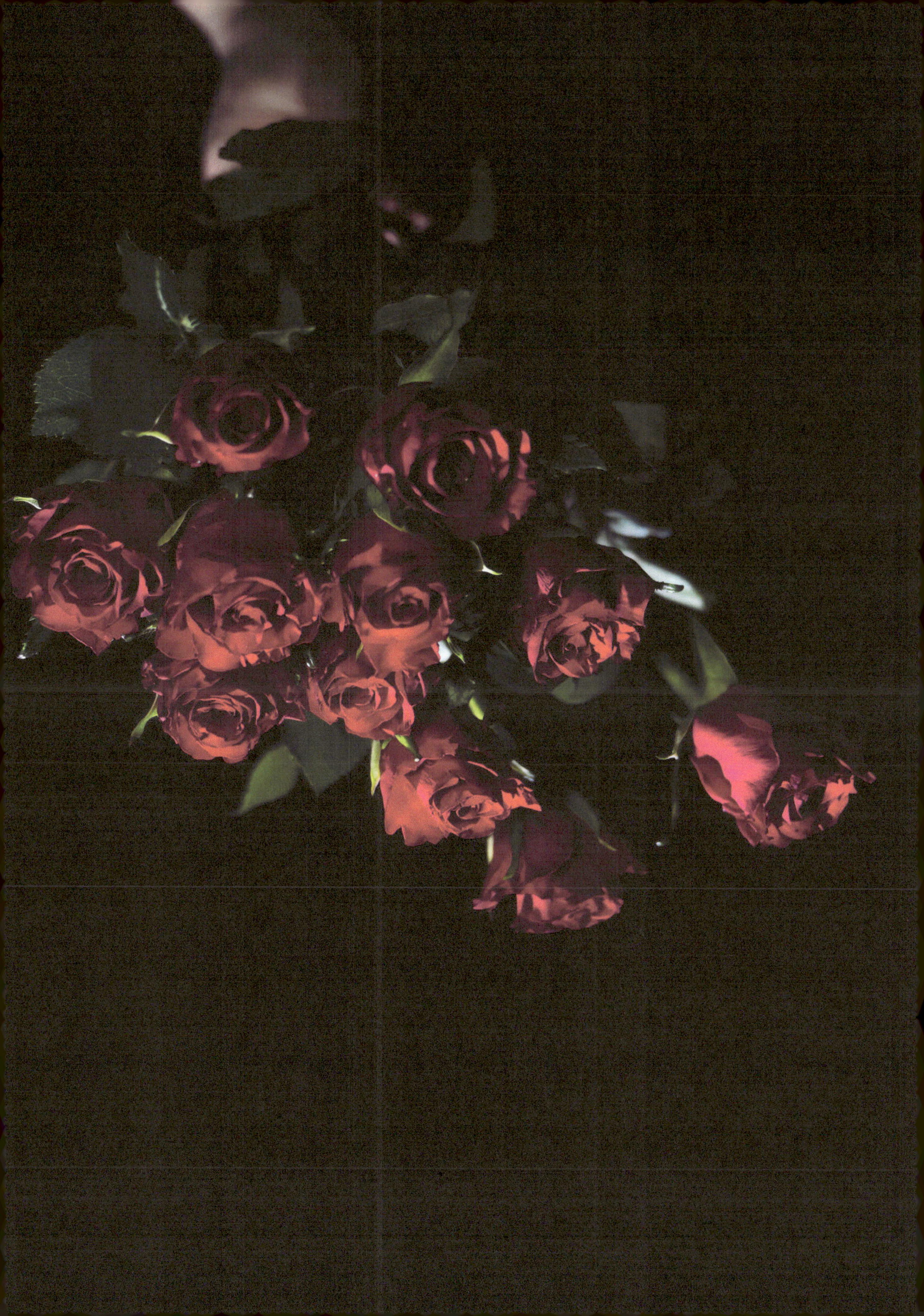

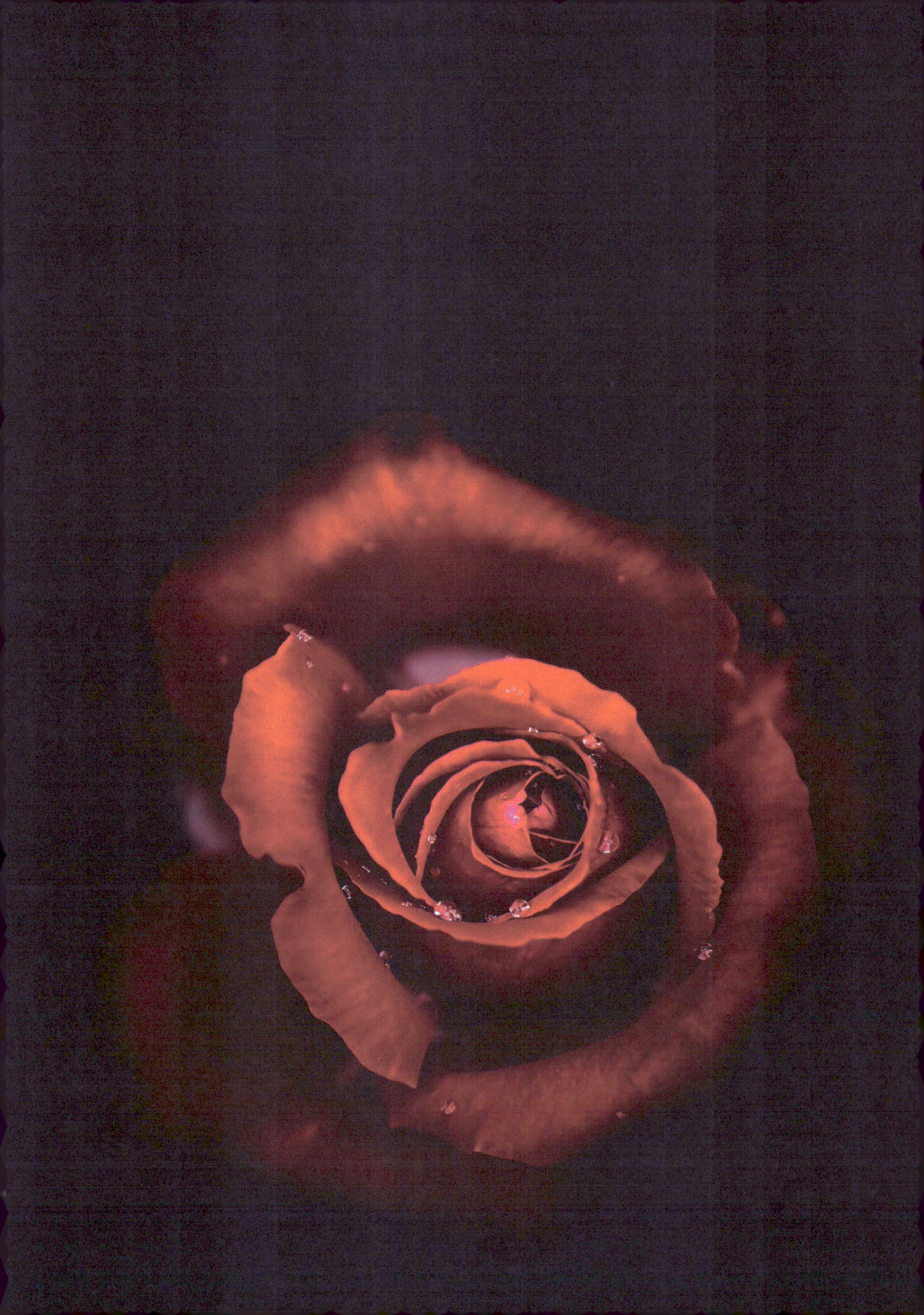

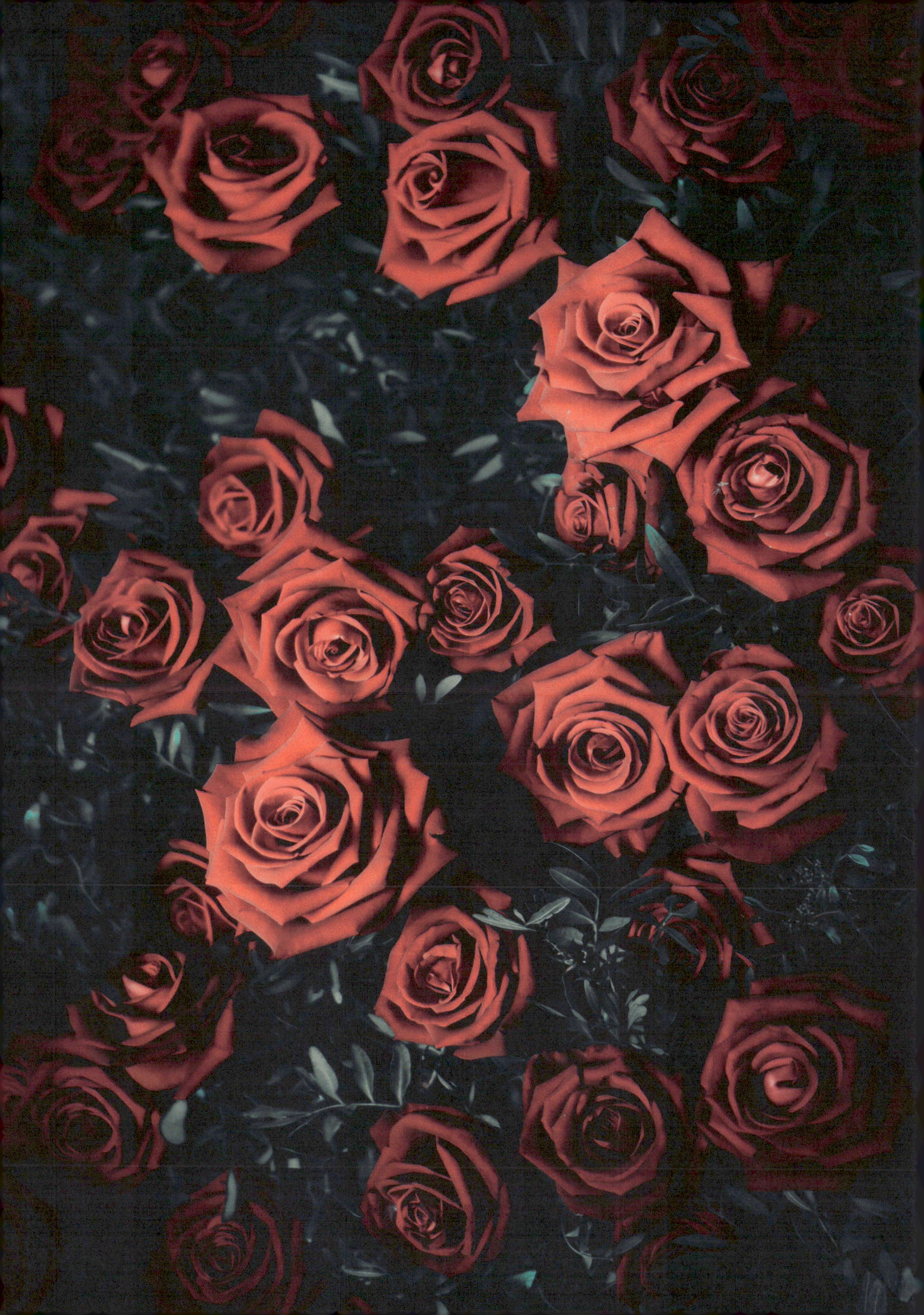

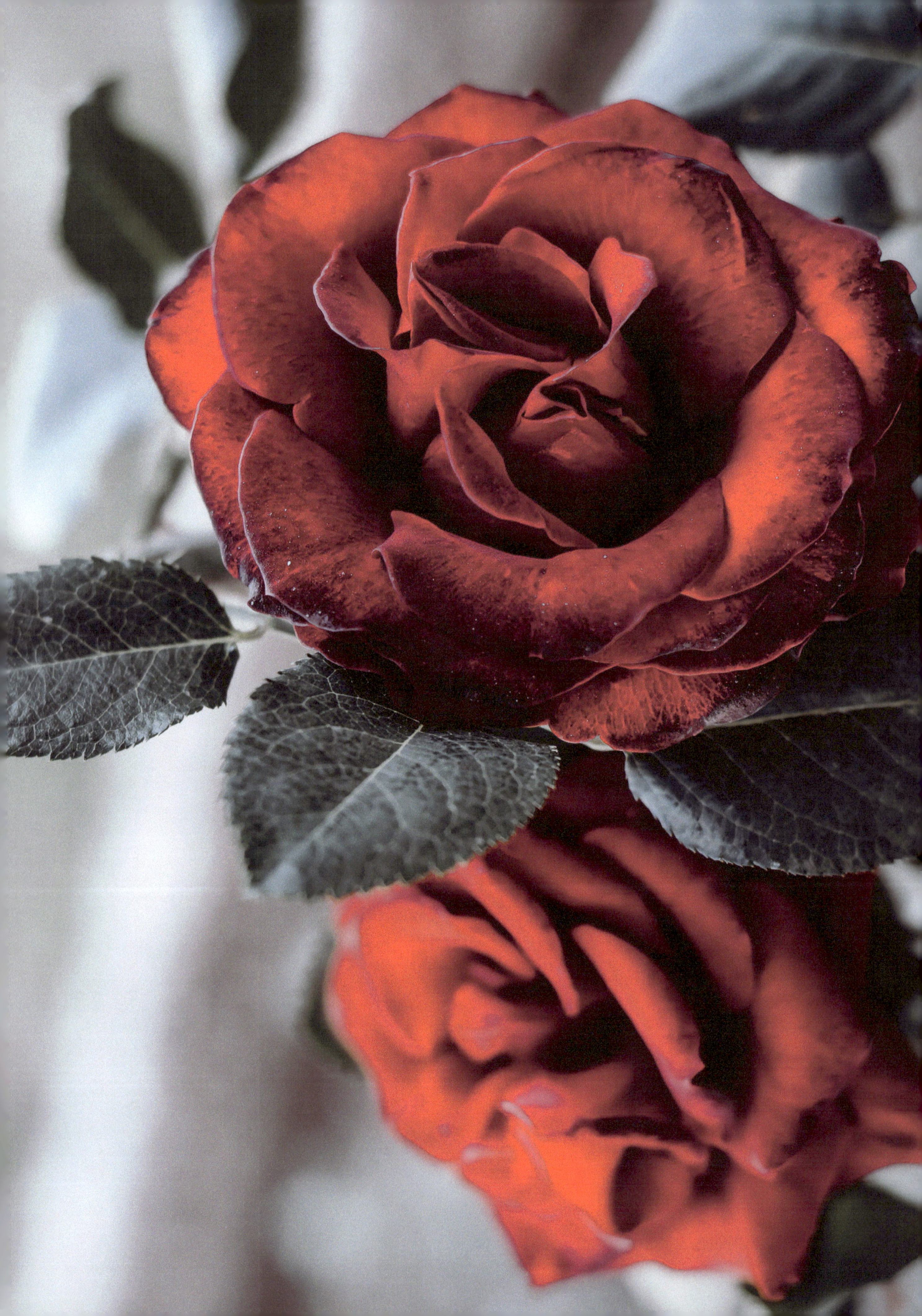

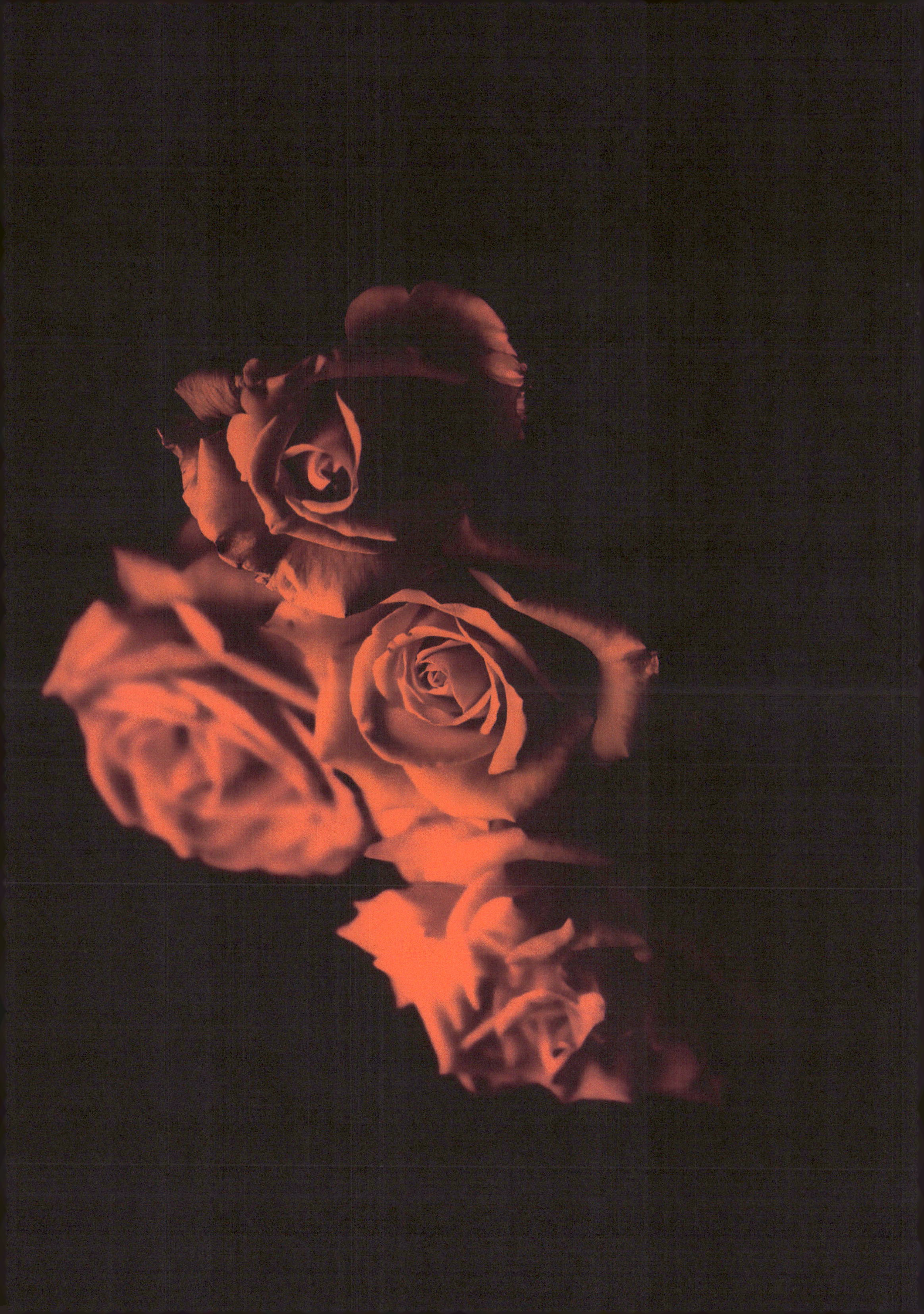

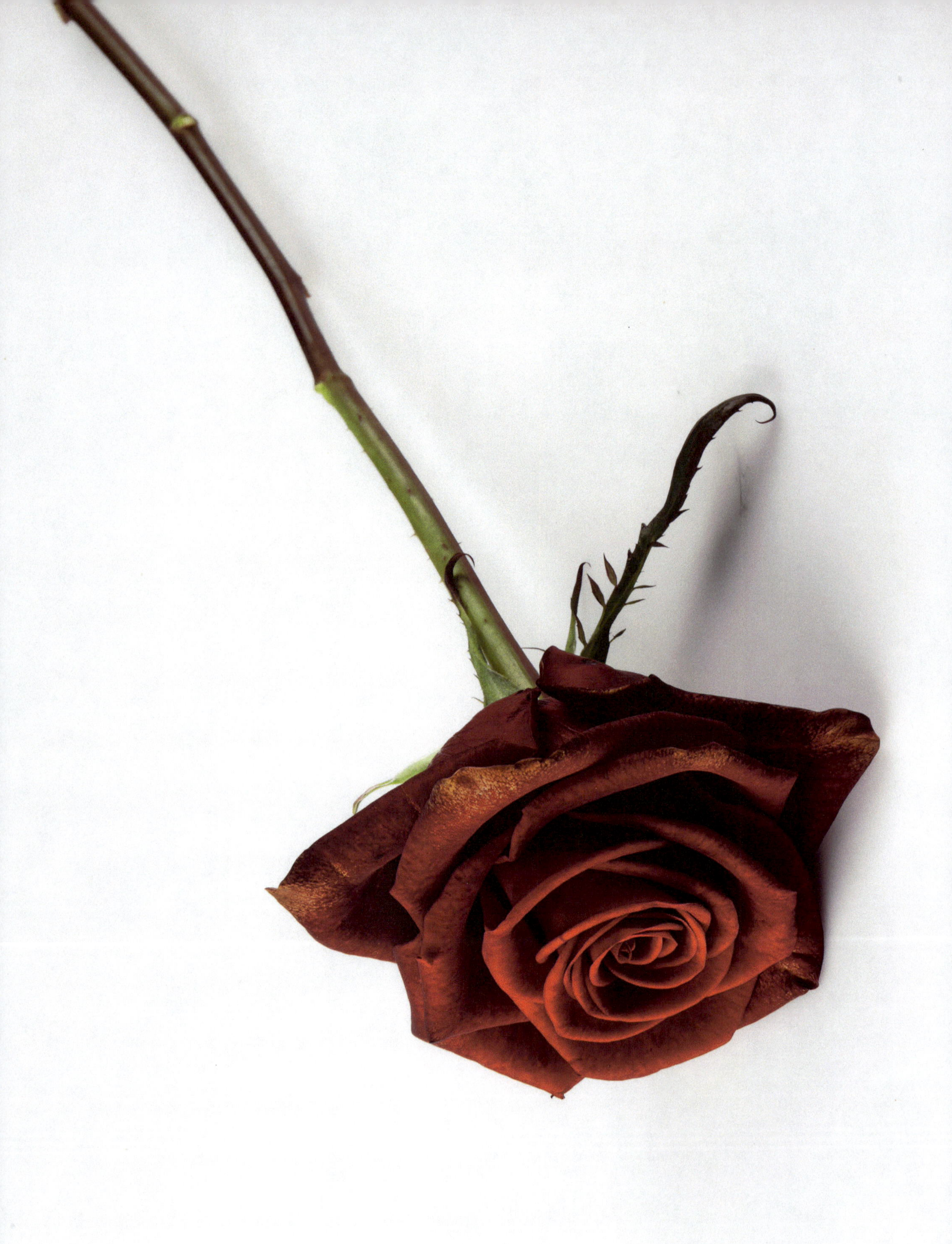

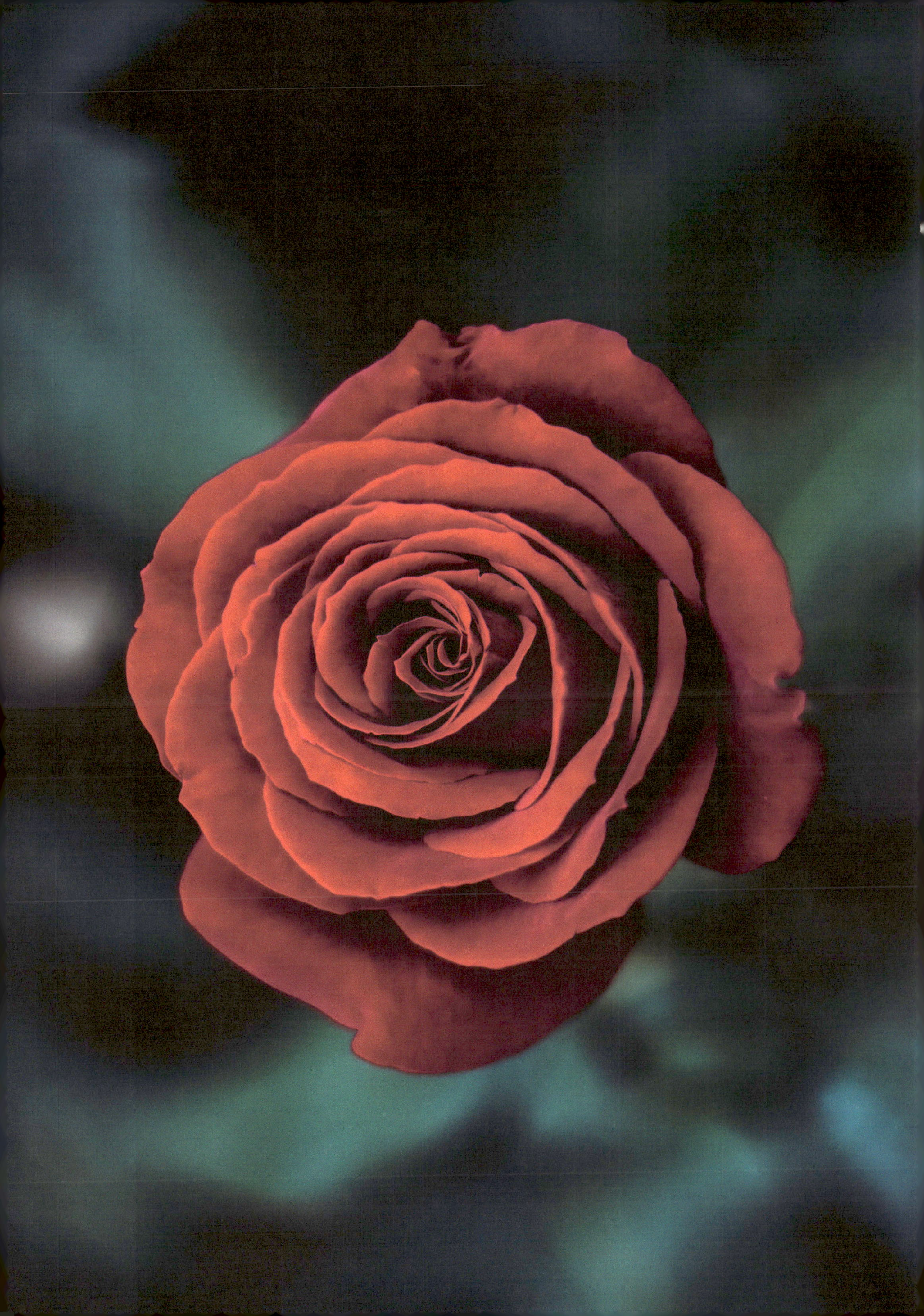

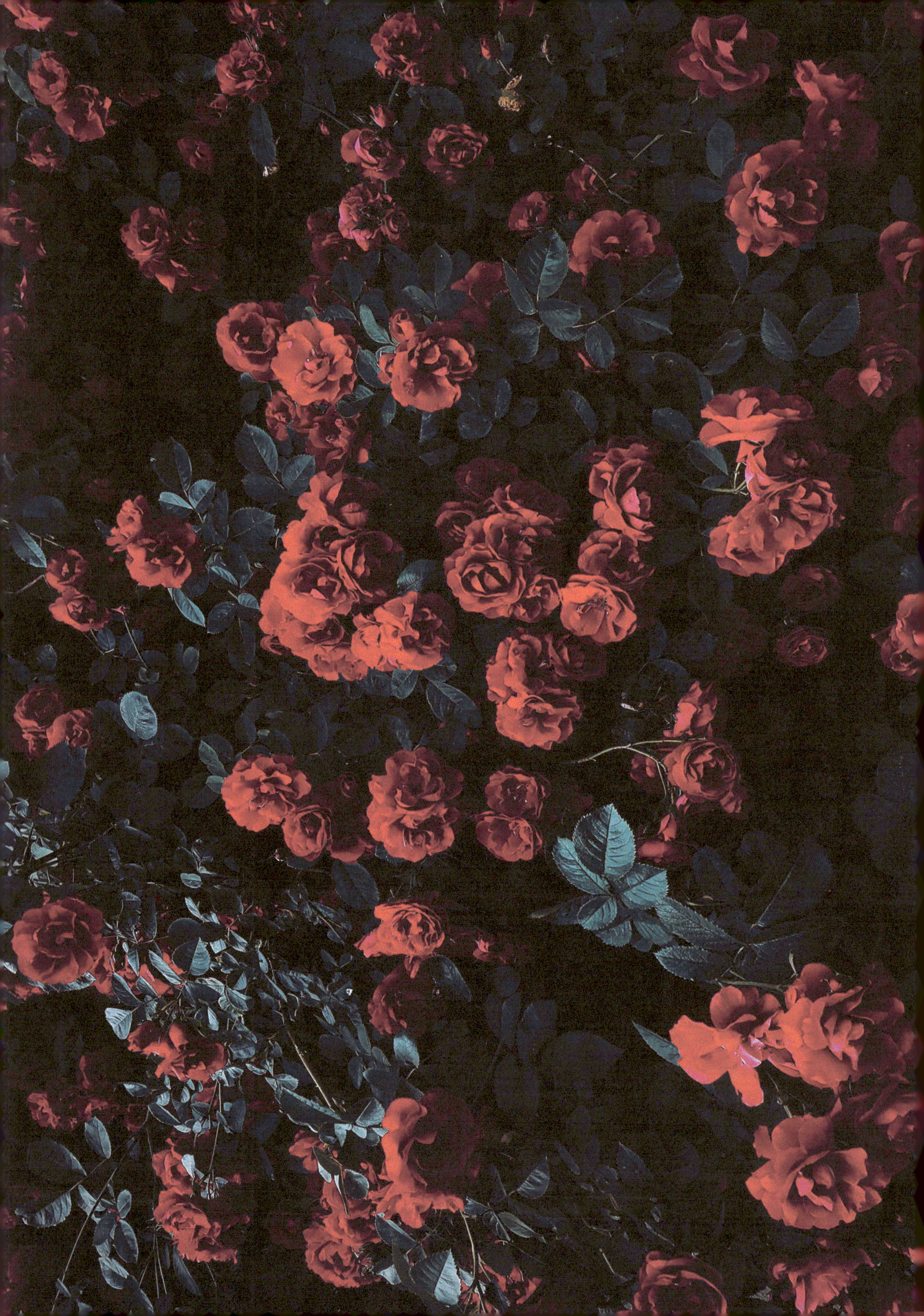

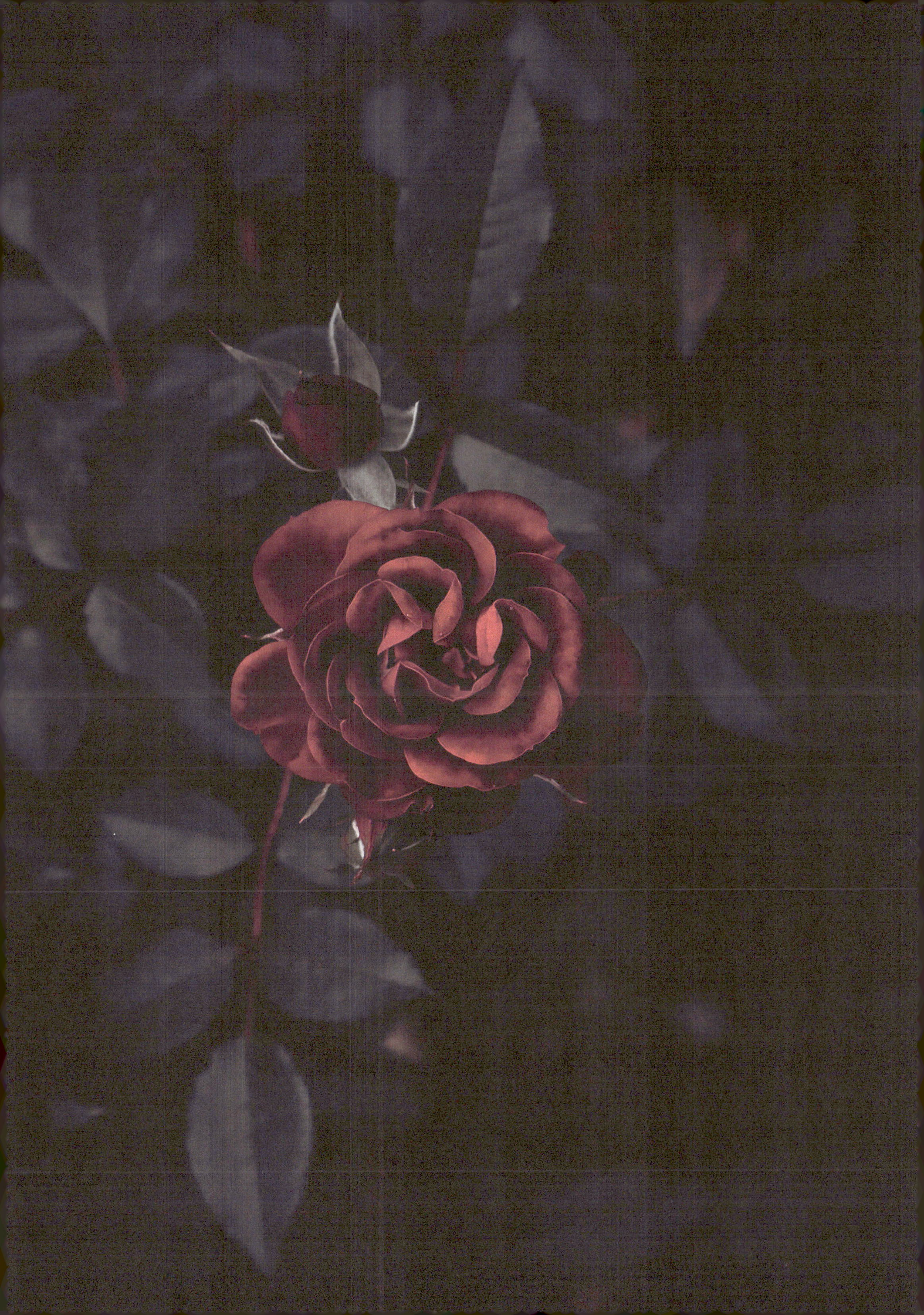

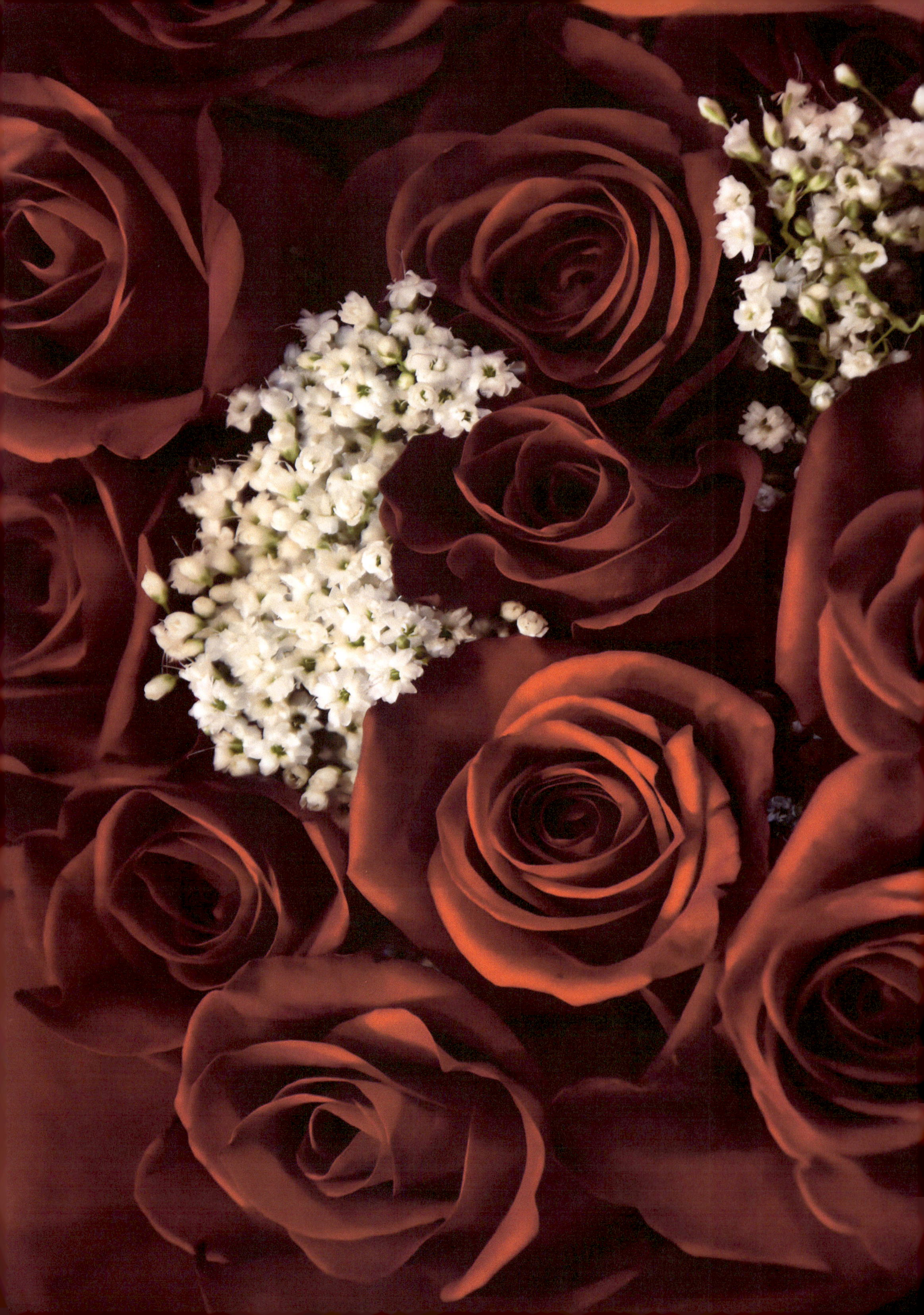

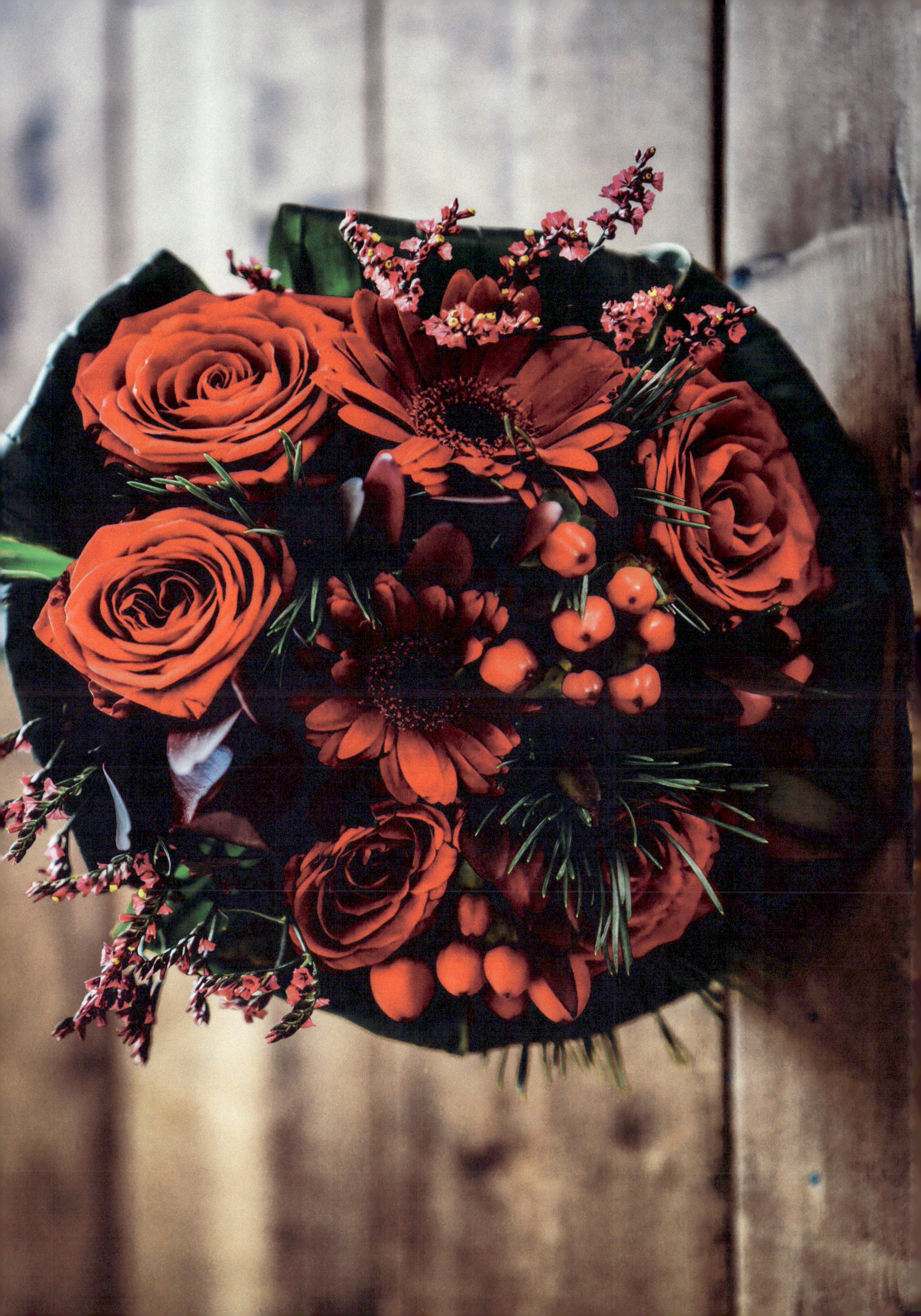

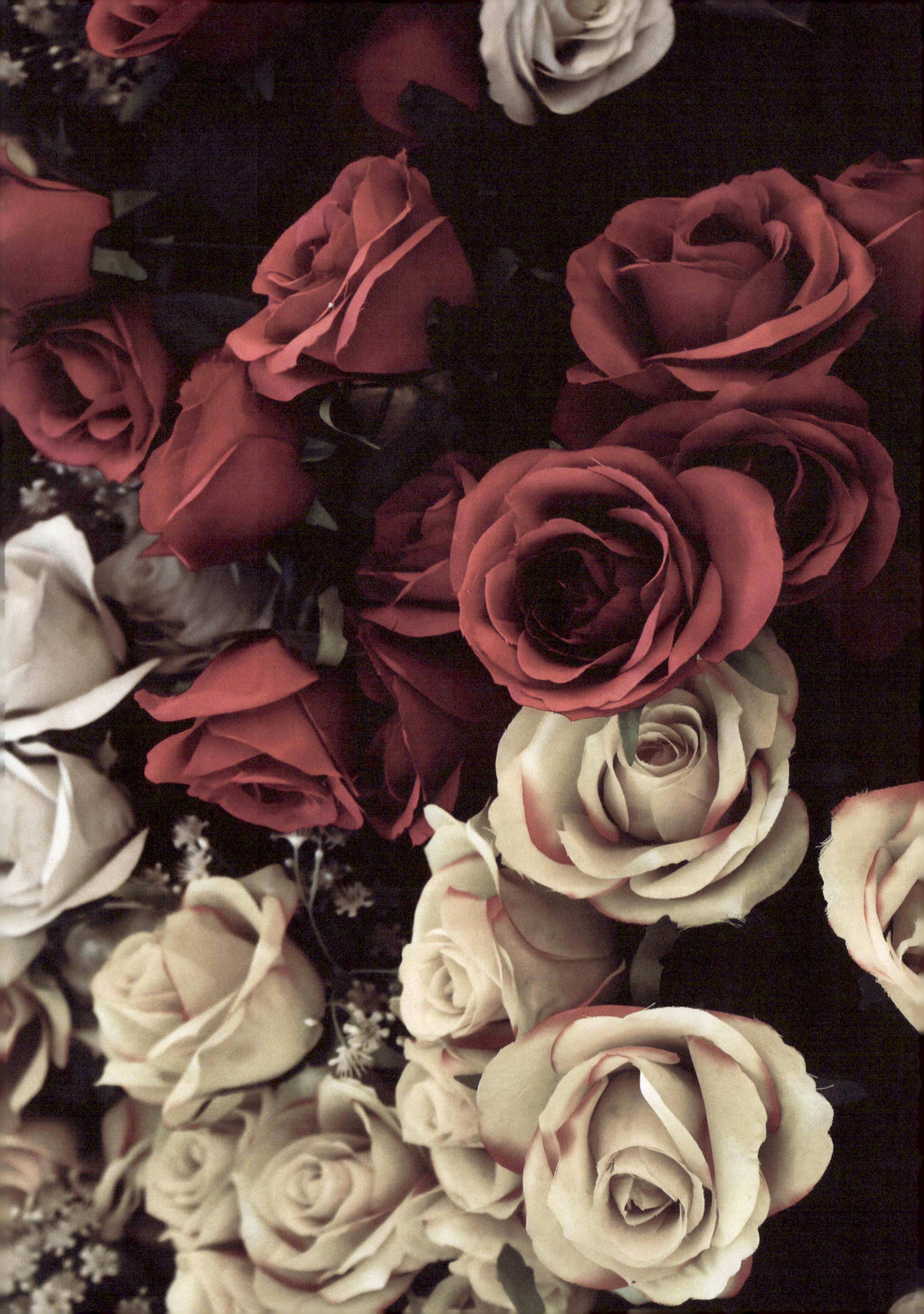

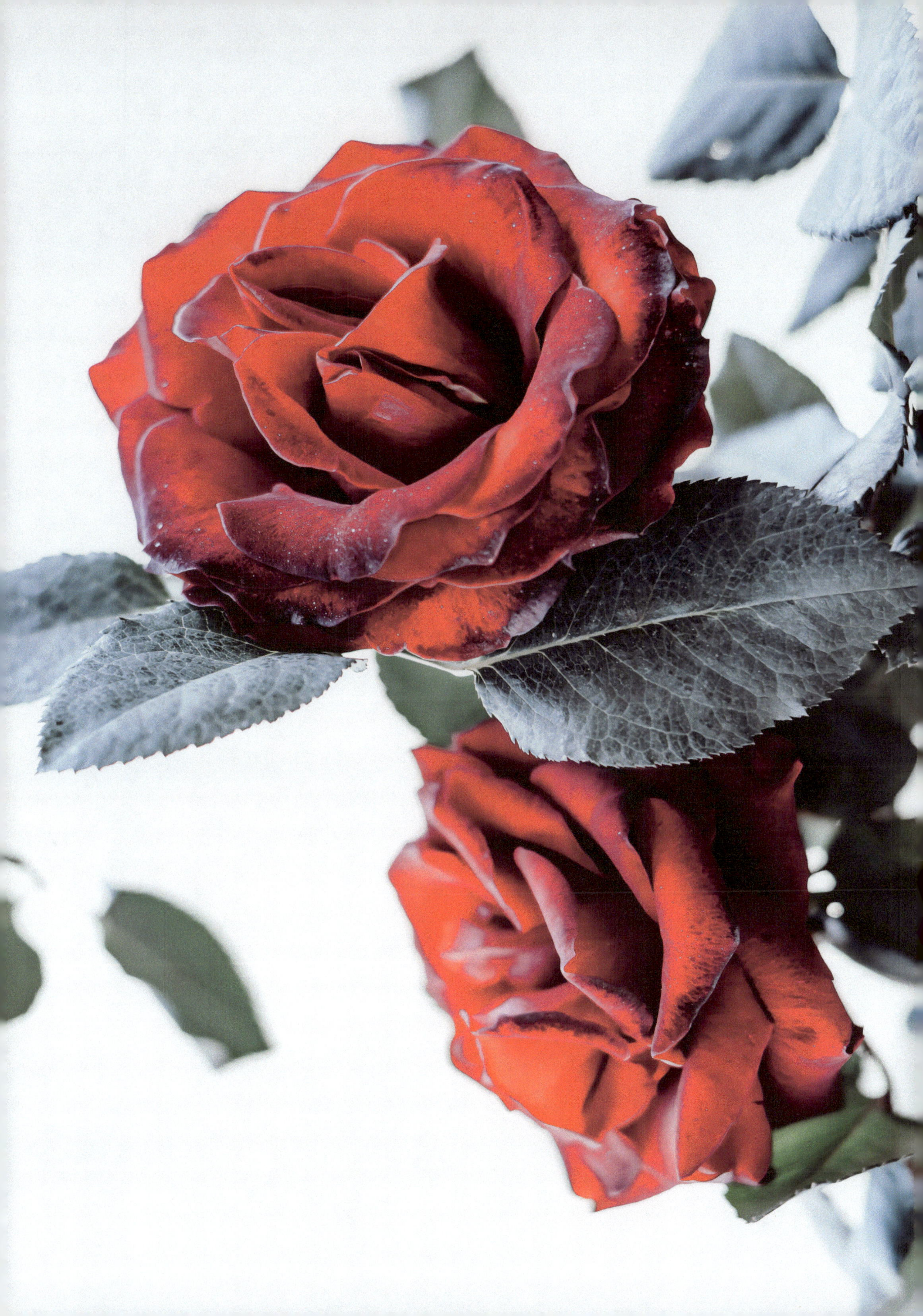

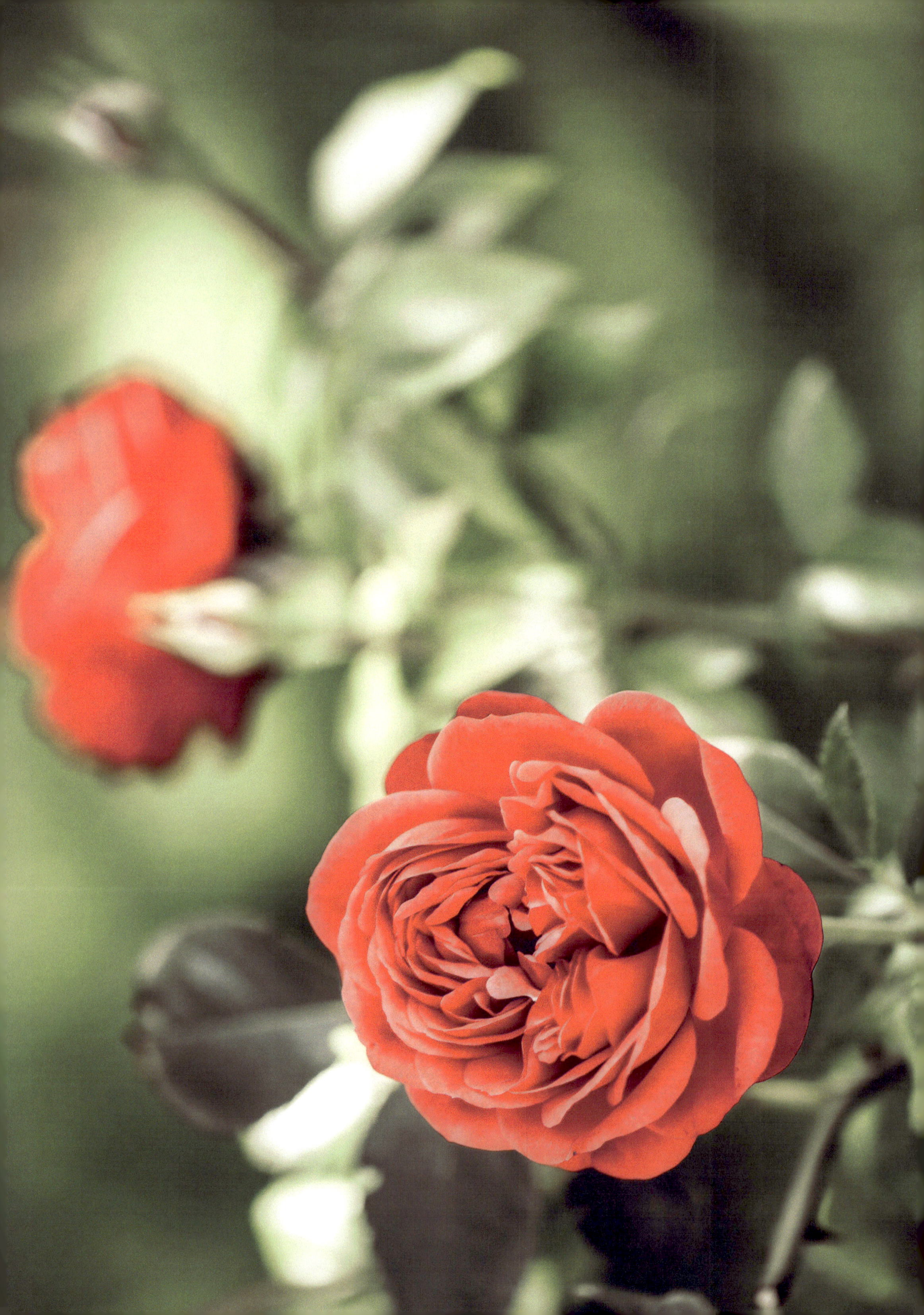

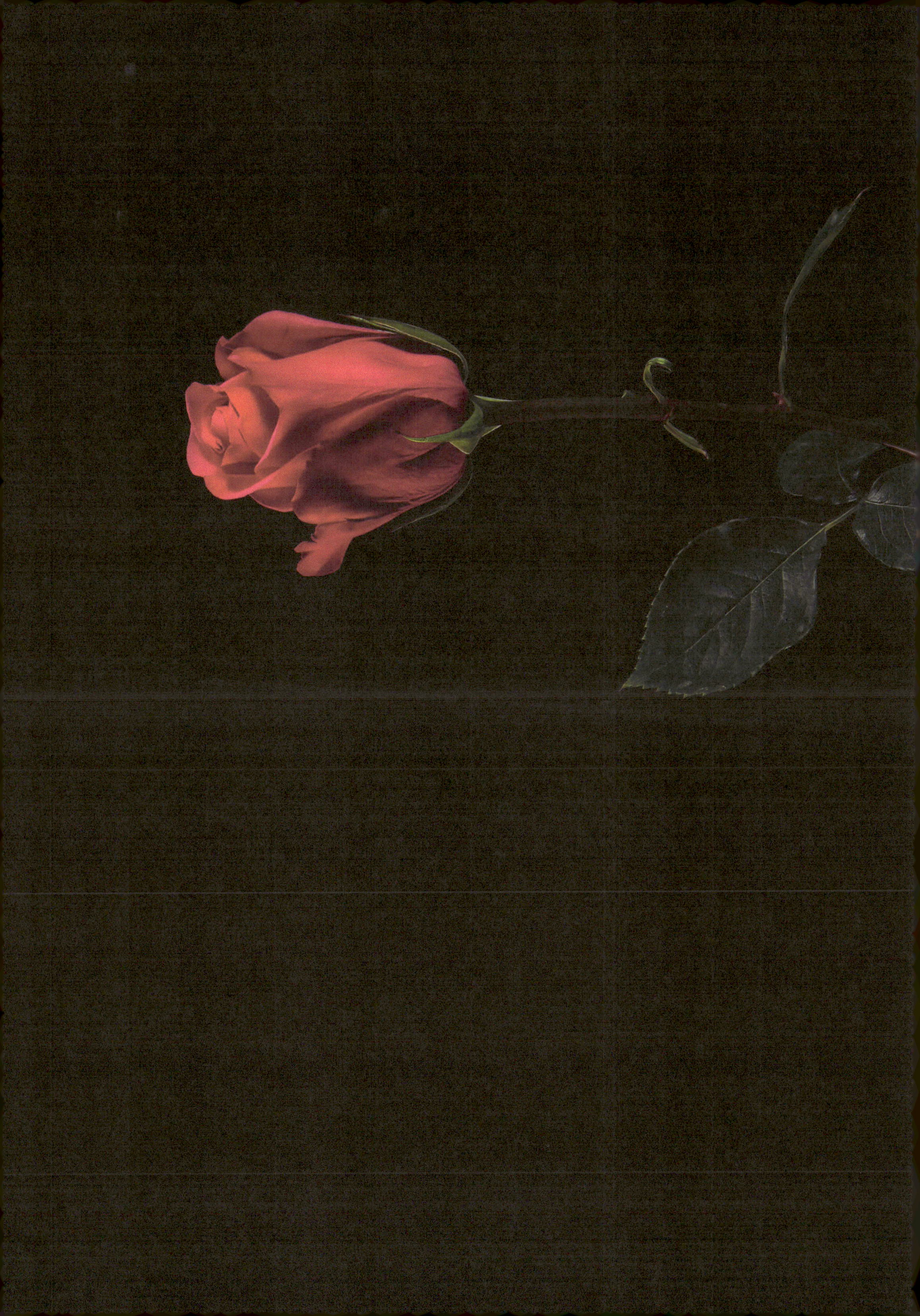

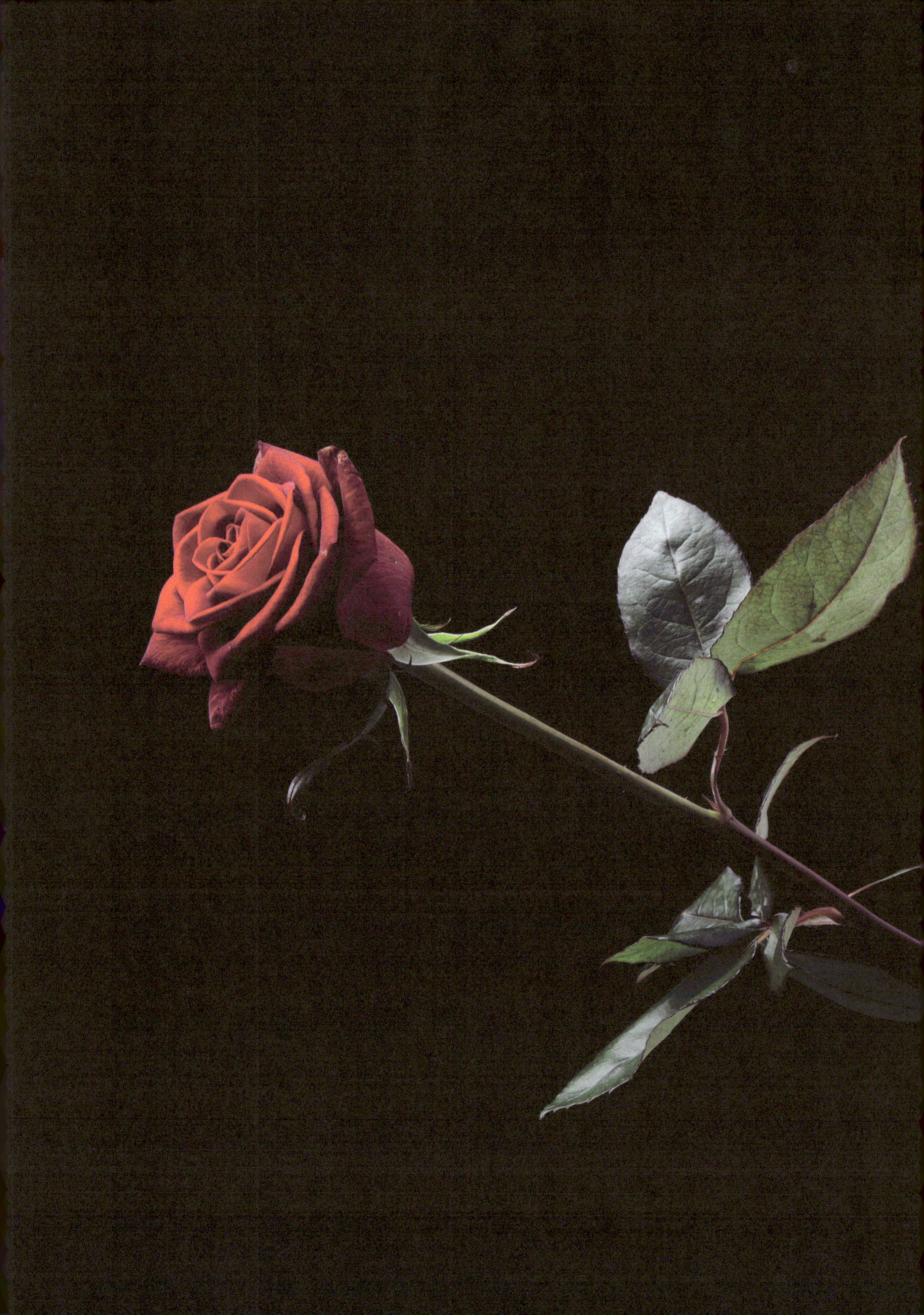

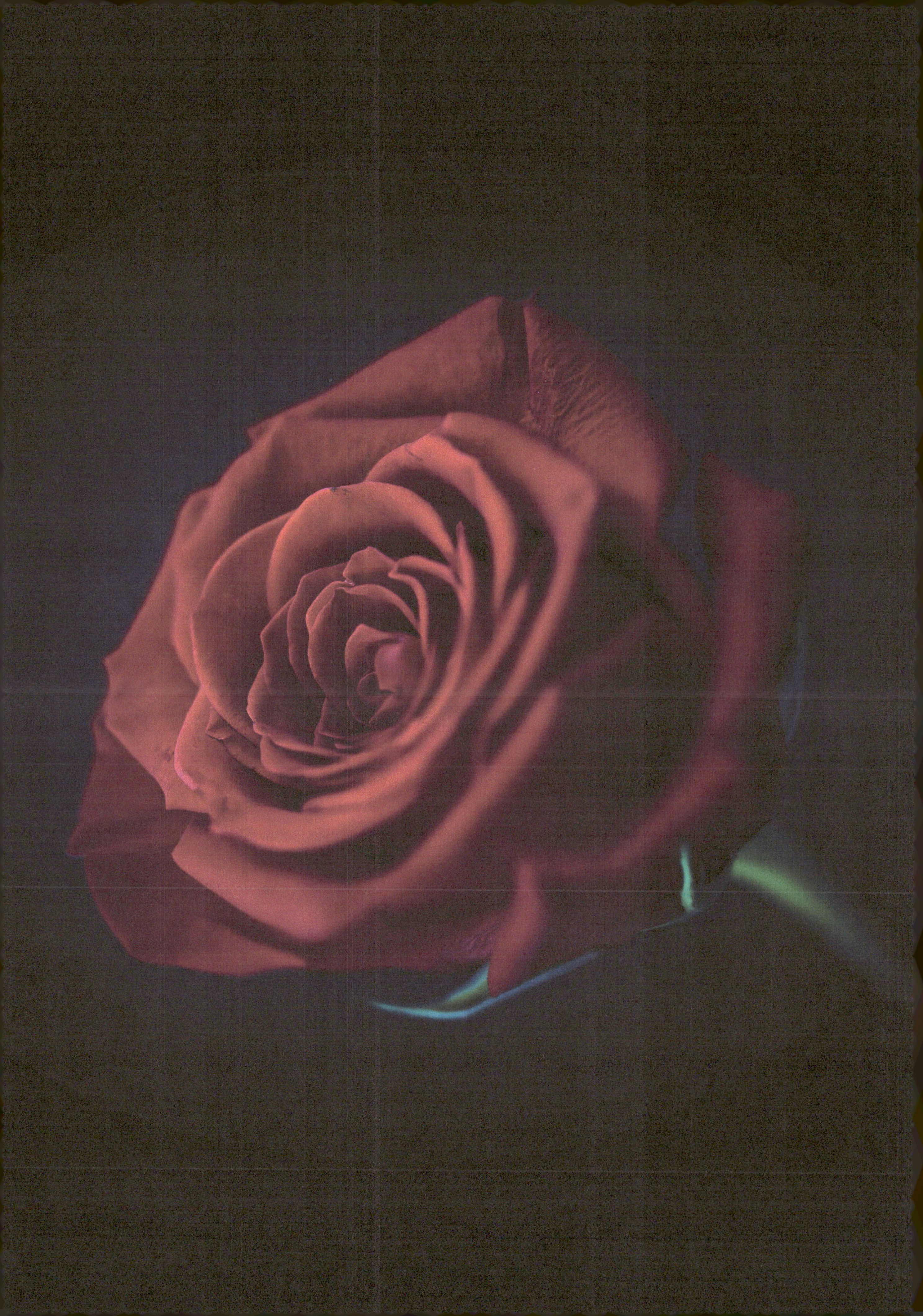

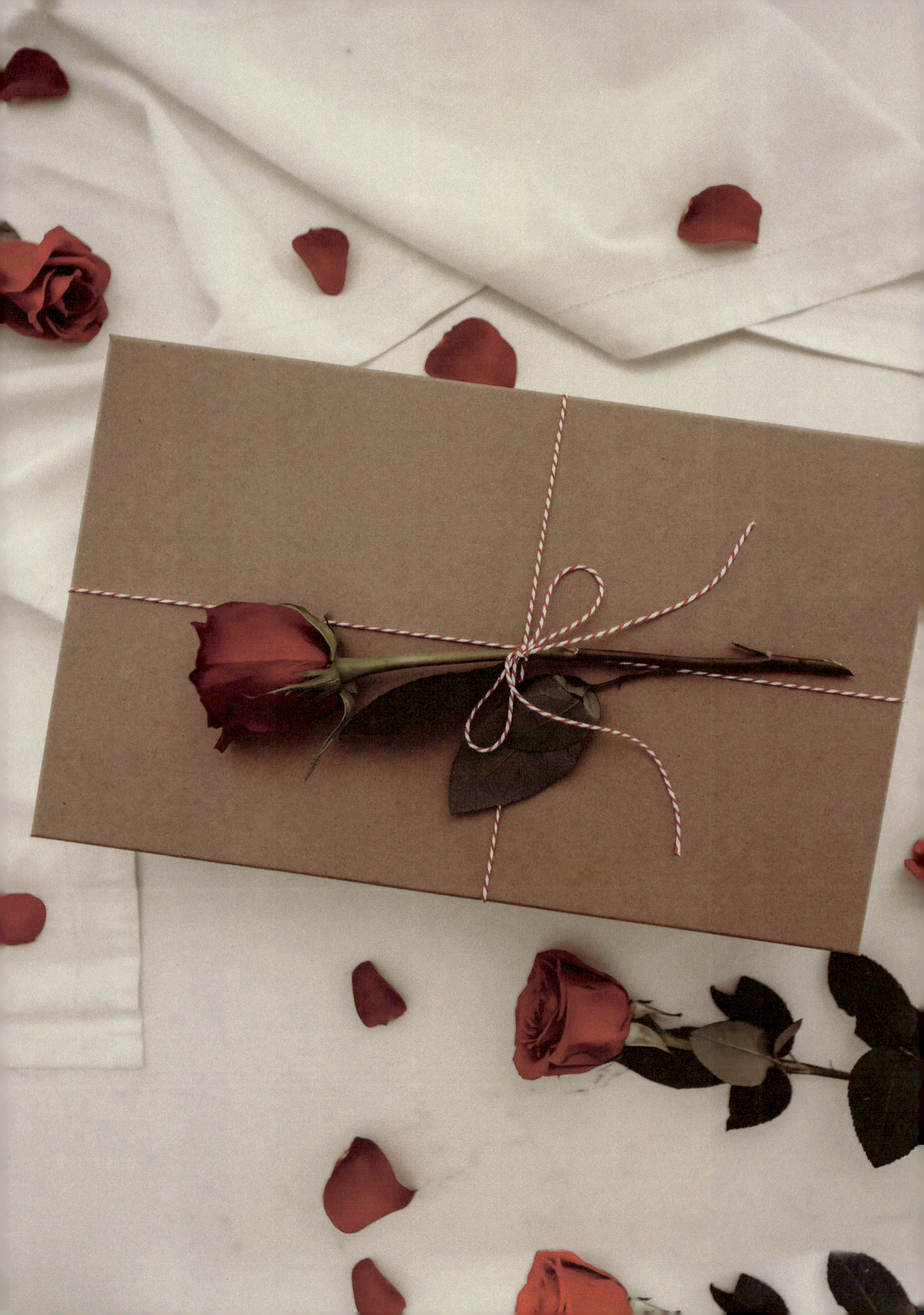

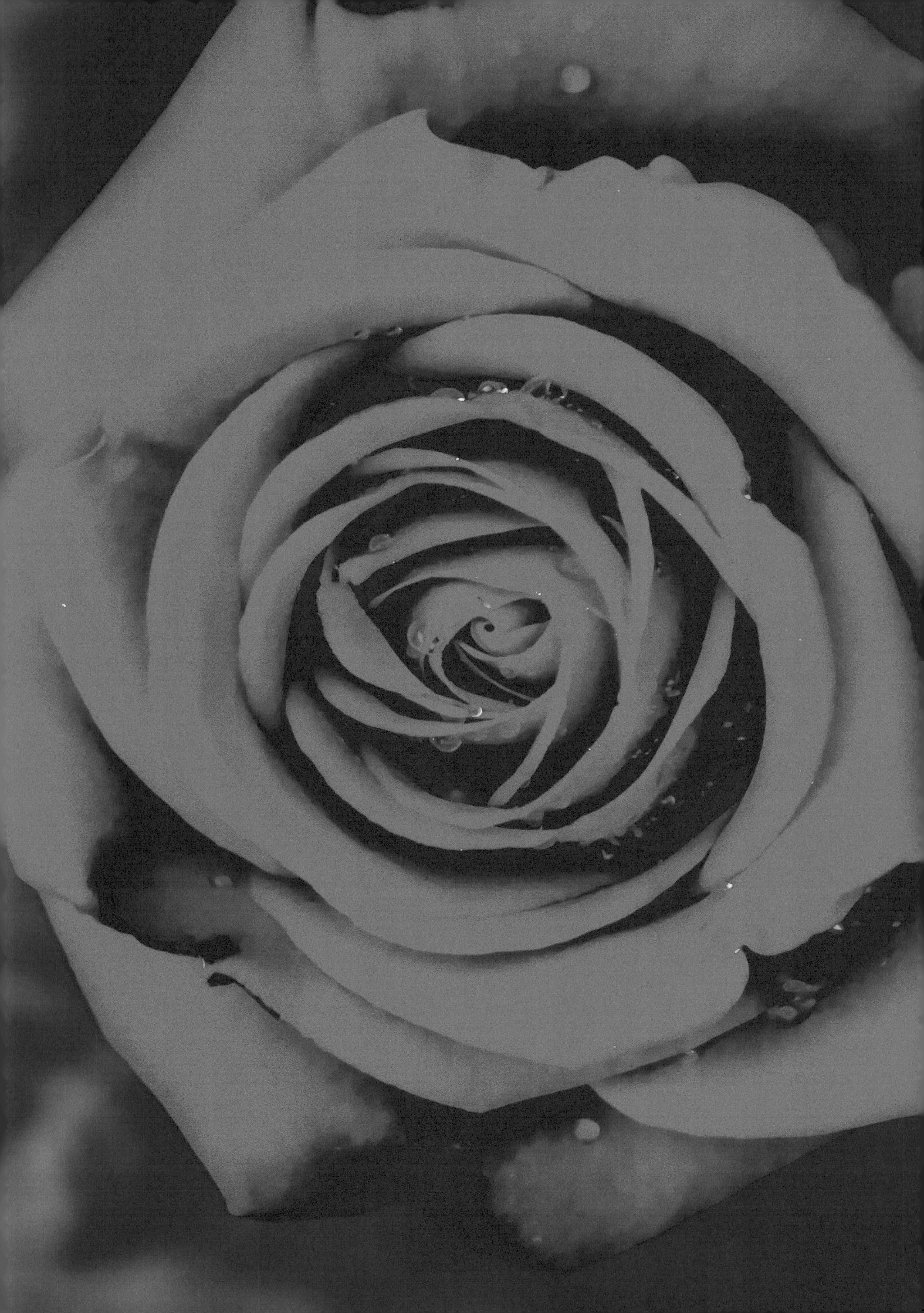

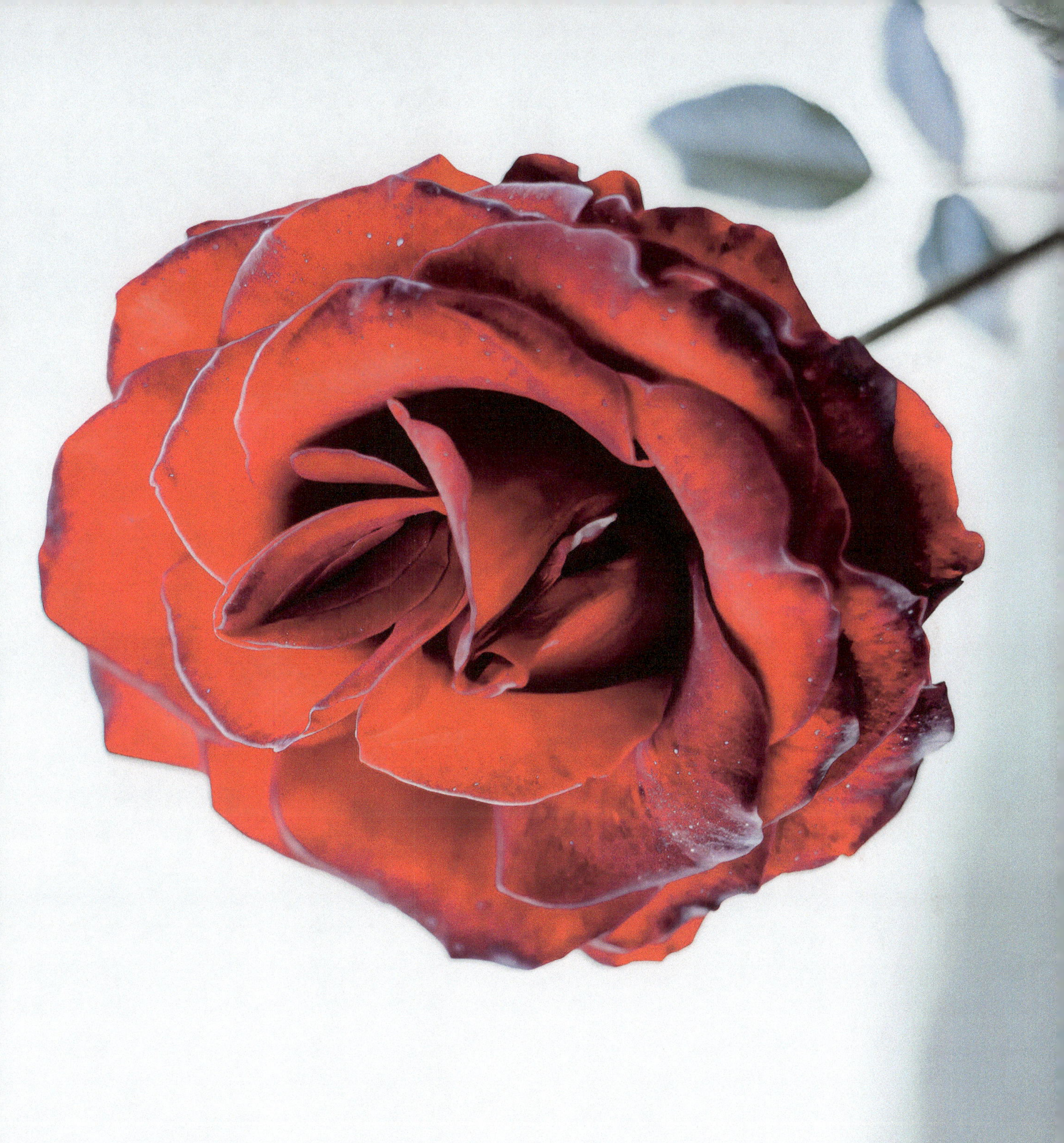

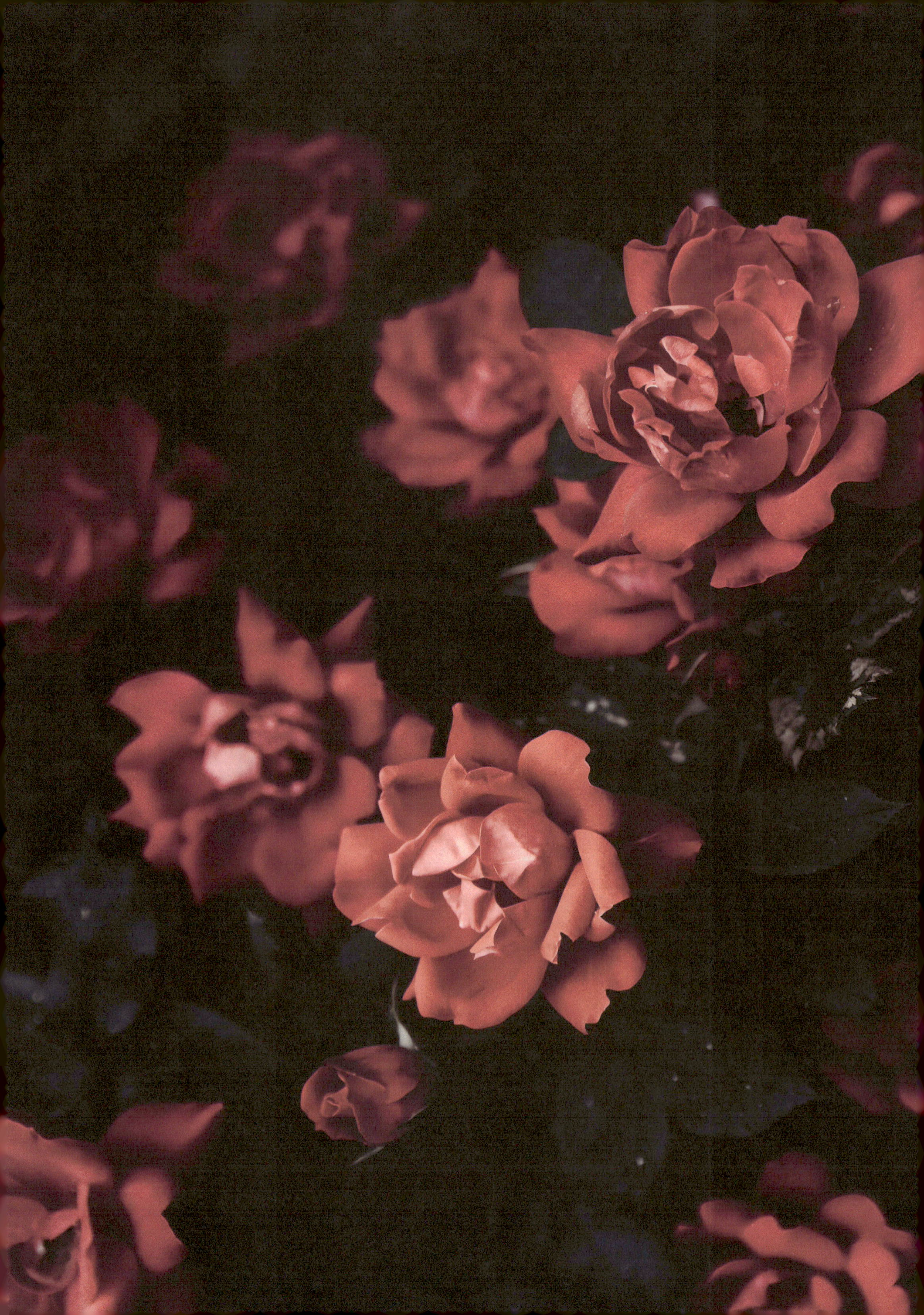

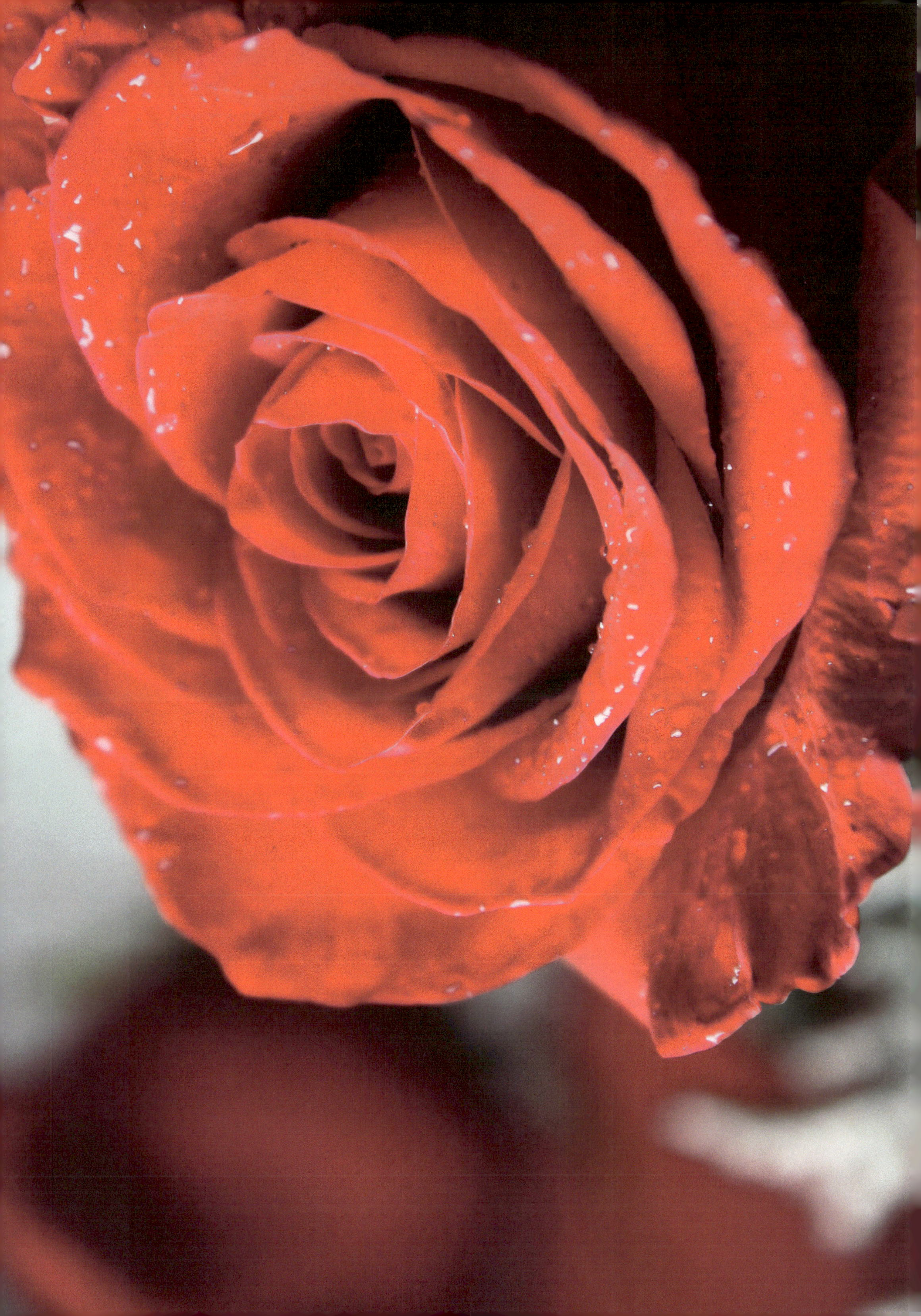

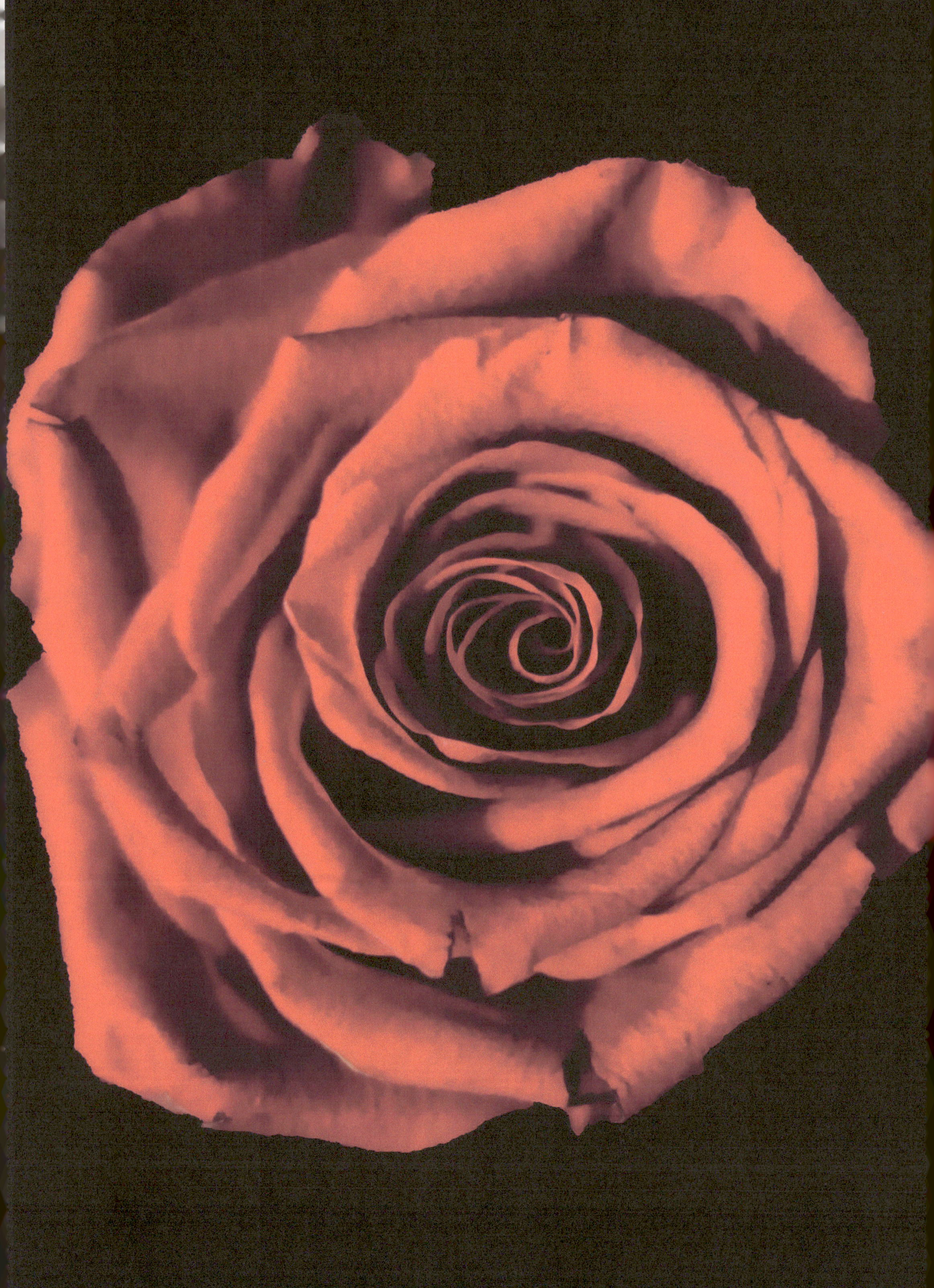

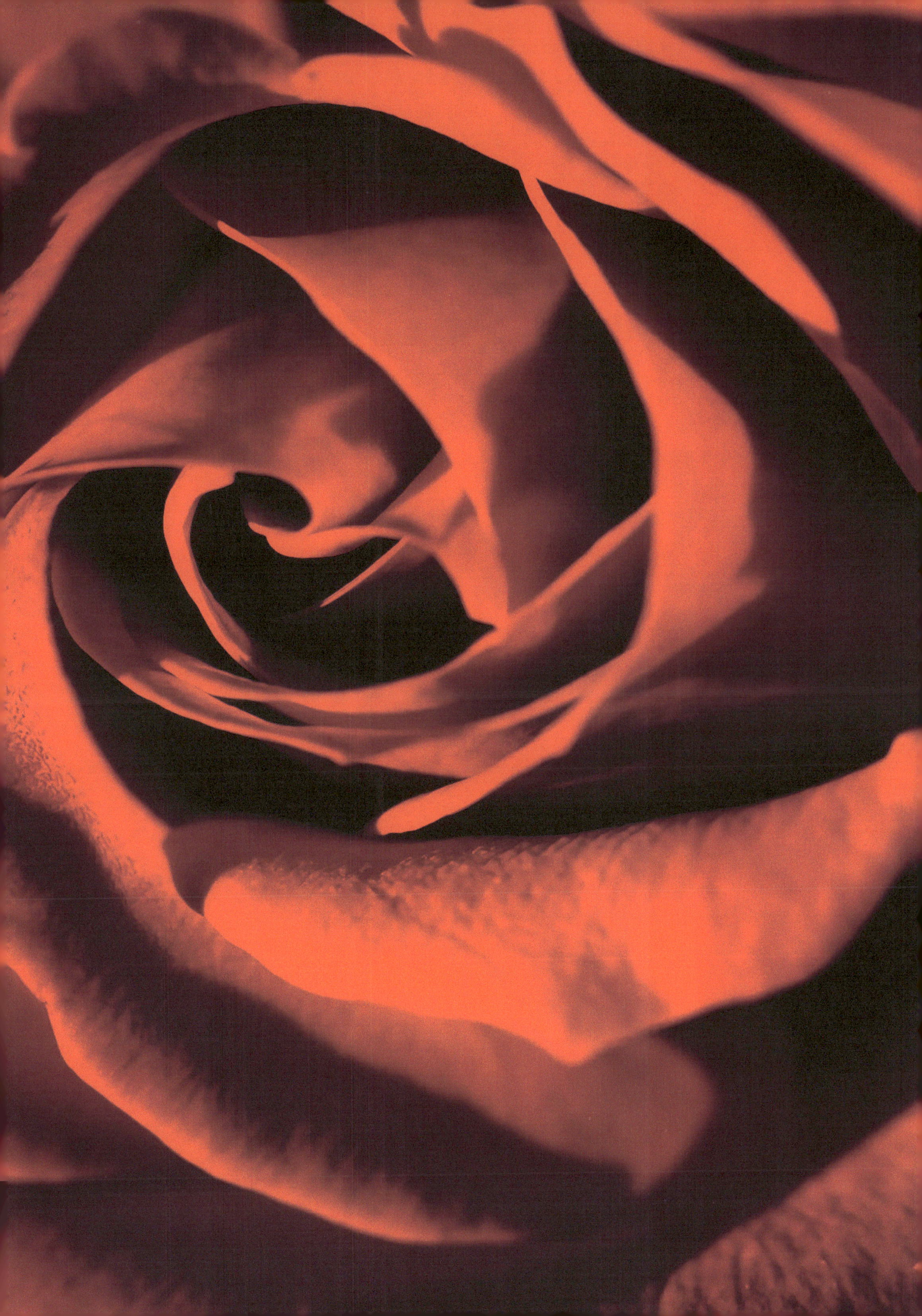

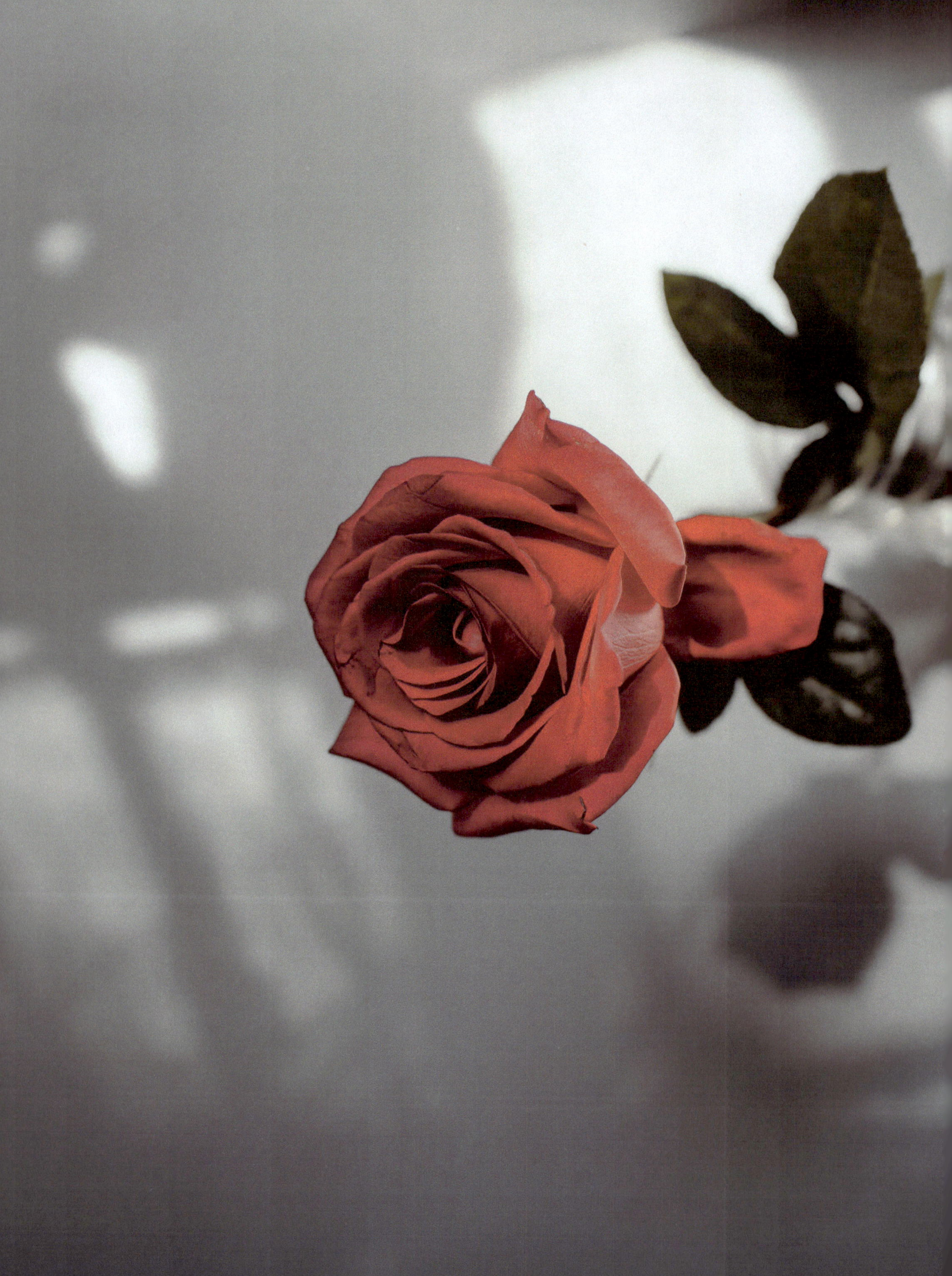

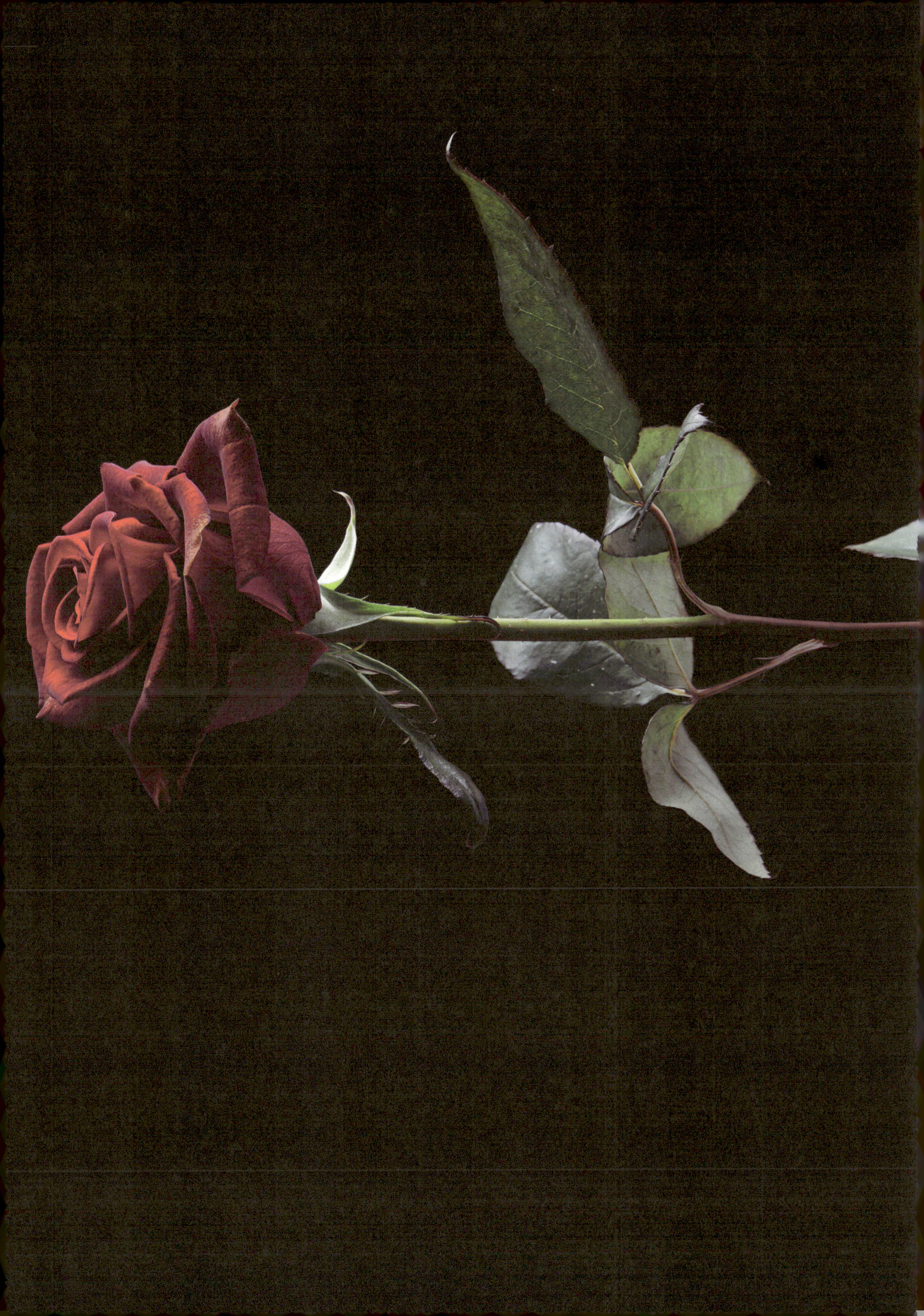

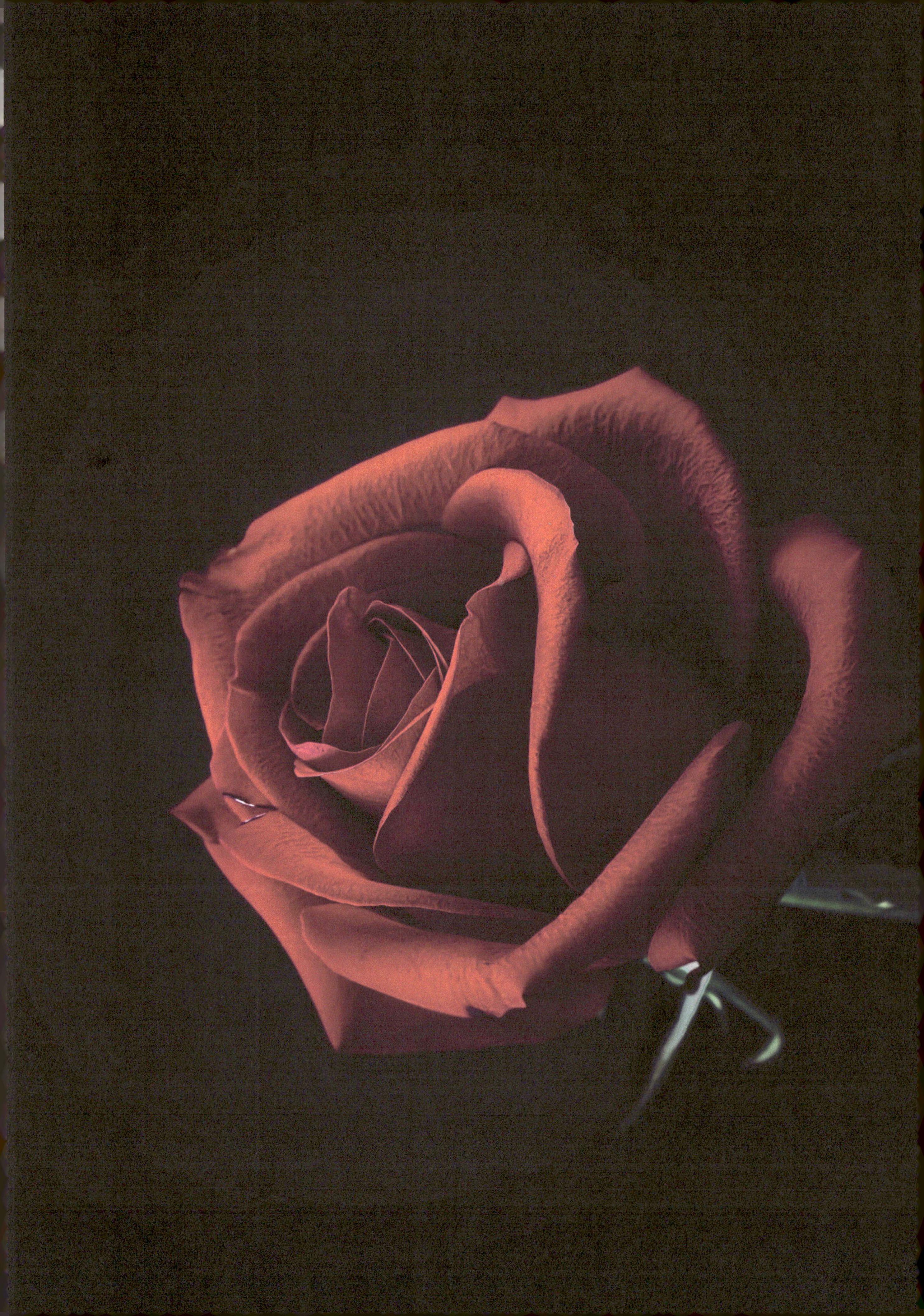

www.ingramcontent.com/pod-product-compliance
Lightning Source LLC
Chambersburg PA
CBHW040211240726
48664CB00002B/915